Farm Girls

201 West Laurel Street

Brainerd, MN 56401

(218) 851-4843

www.RiverPlace-mn.com

ISBN #978-0-9831785-7-6

Printed in the United States of America

Publication date January 2013

Cover Photo:

Luke Borkenhagen

lukeborkenhagen@gmail.com

To our siblings ~
Linda,
Claudia,
& Frank

Farm Girls

Contents

Where I'm From 7

Third Cousins in Norway 8

Galloping to America 9

Primogeniture 10

They Roared in with the Flappers 12

Uncle Louie 13

45 rpm 14

Goodnight Irene 15

Drought 16

Dirt 17

Dry Spell 18

Clothesline Cowboys 18

Radio Preacher 19

Devil in the Details 20

Curtains 21

Last Year of Rural School 23

My Father's Hat 24

Washing My Father's Hair 25

In the Middle of the Night 26

Wonderland 26

Planting Time (A Sestina) 27

Calling the Names 30-31

On Oprah's Couch 32-33

Farm Girls Know 35

Child of Asthma 36

Last Child 37

The Farmer's Daughters 38-39

Secret 42

Prairie 43

Lilac Time 43

Letting Go 44

You Never Know 44

Recipe for Soup 45

Mother with Alzheimer's 46

Mother's Day 2011 46

We Waited Too Long 47

Still in the Game 48

Living Breath, Dying Breath 49

Barn Coats 50

Kingdom 52-53

Acknowledgements 55

About the Authors 56

WHERE I'M FROM

I'm from butchering hens in the forenoon and eating fried chicken for supper. Once a week baths and the old upright piano with the middle C that clanged an empty thump. From forenoon coffee and afternoon chores. Dinner at noon and supper after milking. Meat and potatoes at every meal. Whole milk fresh from the bulk tank, cream rising to the top. From fried bacon, fried ham, fried steak, fried eggs, fried potatoes and Mom's homemade doughnuts. Beet pickles, head cheese, pickled pigs feet, dumpling soup, and cream and bread with a little sugar sprinkled on top. From cooking for threshers and cooking for silo fillers. *Crik*, not creek. *Swatter*, not swather. *Warsh*, not wash. *Not'n*, not nothing. From Norwegian swear words and a grandpa who drank, covering the smell with Sen-Sen candies. From Auntie Ruby with her tightly curled haired and house dresses, who pinched my cheeks with hands so chapped it hurt. From Great-Uncle Louie who chewed snus and always stuck out his finger for me to pull and fat Grandma Inga who warned me not to. I'm from lefse, krumkake and rhubarb gritty with soil, sour in my mouth. Ripe wheat chewed into gum. Apple pies, mud pies, and cow pies. The smell of manure and the suck of a baby calf's mouth. From hay bales that made you sneeze and straw of pure gold. From "Come Boss!" to the cows and "Sic 'em" to the dog. A two-holer outhouse and a one room school house. Pump-Pump Pullaway, Red-Rover, Red-Rover, and Anti-I-Over. Climbing trees, skipping stones and hopscotch. From green hills and pastures spotted with hardwoods and rocks the size of melons heaved up in the soil. From dirt, dark as blackstrap molasses and crops sprouting like new hair in the spring fields. From coffee in a jar carried barefoot through the fields to my father's waiting hands. From salt and sweat and dirt-creased skin. From all of this. From home.

Angela F. Foster

Third Cousins in Norway

I would have been the one who stayed
behind. Timid, afraid of oceans
choosing familiar over precarious
caring for parents and sickly aunts
safer than uncertain wilderness

I would have written letters
with news of deaths or sickness
births and weddings
tucked pansy seeds inside envelopes
to homesick brothers on North Dakota
prairies and Minnesota pineries
read their stories from afar, stroking
blond curls of nephews' hair
pressing their locks to my lips
knowing I would never see their faces

I would have been the last of my
generation left in Norway
the only one to speak with tenderness
connect a face with names, share memories from childhood
answer questions why they left and what they gained
or lost by leaving

I would be the one standing on the other side
of the door, flatbread and lefse baked and waiting
hand-woven cloth with Hardanger lace
reindeer sausage, gjetost brown cheese
everything to perfection

Welcoming distant cousins from America
astonished they could travel so far
yet find their way home

Candace Simar

GALLOPING TO AMERICA

I would have been
the dreamer, scoffing
at my sister's fear.
Naming her ignorant.
Unimaginative. Boring.

I would have counted my kroners
hoarding them as dreams.
Ironing for the Nobleman's widow.
Sitting in childbed for the neighbor.
Never spending on dresses or foolery.
Saving, always saving,
building passage to America.

I would have waved away my mother's
clutching hands. Refused to practice
the Hardanger lace stitches. Scorned
the work of women. Learned to plant
and harvest fields. Spent time

teaching my tongue
the strange English words.

I would have painted my name on a travel
trunk sturdy enough to cross oceans
and the sea of prairie. Folded and packed
the fine linens stitched for my dowry.
Filled the empty spaces with the practical—
aprons, metal pots, seeds for the new land,
imagining black ribbons behind my plow.

I would have pushed aside
offers of marriage from timid men.
Scorned their thin arms.
Dreamed instead of a Viking.
Broad shouldered.
Adventurous enough
to cross the seas.

I would have longed
for blond haired sons
bold like their father
who would push the plow
and protect the homestead.
And daughters
tall and lithe, who would
marry into money.

In my daydreams we prospered.
Letters home bragged of riches.
Servants no more. Landowners.

In my night dreams I sailed
across the seas. My phantom
husband beside me, galloping
the ocean waves, our faces turned
toward America.

Angela F. Foster

PRIMOGENITURE

In the earliest wave of second-born sons
Great-grandfather left this Norwegian mountain
Odelsgaard, ancestral farm, destined for first-born

Pushed to a nation with land
for all the world's sons
place blooded by Civil War
desperate *Red Men* forced back

What thoughts he carried
as he left *mor* and *far*, brothers and sweetheart
shook dust from feet to travel the route of Columbus
thirty-six long days aboard the *White Dove*
at the mercy of the sea

He turned his heel and walked away from this village
where sheep graze fields so steep men bind
themselves with ropes to scythe the hay.
He left this churchyard where his sister slept
beside grandparents, great-grandparents
home for our family since 1348
when Black Death killed half of Norway

How could he
cut the binding ropes
never to return?

Candace Simar

THEY ROARED IN WITH THE FLAPPERS

Rode prosperity after the Great War
weathered the Dirty 30s, a scorching storm
suffered prohibition, didn't complain
and placed their dreams on hold
to free the world from fascism

Then married and their babies boomed

Super power now—a slippery perch
Berlin airlift and cold war in Korea
they embraced Alaska and Hawaii
rocketed to the moon

but still their parents aged and died

They grieved their loss as children
protested Viet Nam and Nixon
bemused by how their fight, so long and hard
lay scorned on silver platters

They kept the faith, the old one of their fathers
and dazed, watched while children
followed Maharishi or freaked
out for Jesus

Retiring with inflation
they rode the 80s Bust as best they could
learned technology in the 90s (or didn't)
Wired, they braced for Y2K that fizzled
old in the new century and weary
they leave us in a steady stream
a tired ripple on the tide of time

Candace Simar

UNCLE LOUIE

Would amble from his little shack at the edge of town and mosey toward the General Store, enjoying the breeze, commenting on the weather and his neighbor's dahlias. He wore bib overalls with a red bandanna handkerchief hanging out of his back pocket. He'd plunk two dimes and three pennies on the worn store counter while Mr. Rorvig plucked a can of Copenhagen from the tube on the wall. Sometimes Uncle Louie added a tin of sardines or ten cents worth of summer sausage. He didn't need much. Didn't want more than he owned. He had an easy life—no wife or job to worry about, freedom to play cards all night or go duck hunting for a week. Chewing, chewing, always chewing, his stubbly chin dribbling bits of tobacco and brown stains. Uncle Louie almost always hit the coffee can spittoon with a perfectly aimed stream. When he was in his eighties, a new preacher asked why he never married. Uncle Louie shrugged. "No one ever asked."

Candace Simar

MAR • 65 •

45 RPM

like black vinyl, our marriage spins
round and round
familiar grooves and melodies
and that spot that always skips
predictable, comfortable

still making music
together after forty-five years

Candace Simar

GOODNIGHT IRENE

Irene Hannah Christine Jensen   1910-1913

The portrait hung over
Grandma's four-poster
bed, the background a white mist.
Wispy blonde hair, black
button boots, eyelet apron
and a folded pocketknife
clutched in her tiny hands.

Irene Hannah Christine—a child
so special she needed
two middle names.

Grandma would sigh
as she told the story
of Irene's short
life, her fevered
face, labored breath.
No penicillin.
No doctors.

Grudging
acceptance. God's
will be done.

Years later whenever
"Goodnight Irene"
would play on the old
Philco radio, Grandma
would sing along
eyes closed

her words a whispered quaver
Goodnight Irene, Goodnight Irene,
I'll see you in my dreams.

Angela F. Foster

Drought

We talked about the weather, the crops, and the cost of gasoline. Complained about taxes, the price of wheat. Every conversation a variation of the same. The women stitched feed sack dresses or embroidered dishtowels and worried about the corn. The men cast anxious glances towards the skies while monkeying with worn down tractors or patching wagons with baling wire. We never talked about feelings, never acknowledged emotions. We commented on how someone was taking a death in the family, bragged about someone who just kept working, the one who refused to let a little thing like death or sickness get him down or set him back. We glossed over the big things and dwelt in smaller places, closer in size to the acreage of our farms. Maybe town people talked about deeper issues. We didn't. When a neighbor shot himself, Auntie Ragna complained at the funeral about the lack of butter on the egg salad sandwiches. *Old lady Norstrom trying to save a penny*, she said. *Always trying to squeeze another nickel out of every dime*. No one mentioned the suicide. No one talked to his boys, red and sodden in their Sunday suits, other than a crisp nod and quick handshake. *They held up real well*, Auntie would say later. *Never shed a tear*.

Candace Simar

DIRT

Dirt—harsh, black
and peppered
with rocks—
stuck to his work
boots like spring gumbo

Green shoots
kept his stubborn
hope alive
a fire licking twigs

He said it a hundred times
  after the rocks are picked
  after planting
  after harvest
next year

Dirt kept him going
long after his body
needed rest
working the fields
all night

On a rusty
John Deere tractor
soil embedded
into the wrinkles
of his skin

Dirt eroded
his health like
a south wind
through a dry
field

In the end
dirt toppled him
in his passing, dirt
welcomed him home

Angela F. Foster

DRY SPELL

A dry spring
for weeks
no rain
the lawn, prickly
as a wire brush

Grasshoppers
lace soybean
leaves, chew
the tender
blades of hay

Daily
I scan
the sky
searching
for clouds

Stunted corn
and a winter
without hay
our only cash crop
fill my thoughts

This last week
of August
rain comes
cracked earth
opens to drink

Overnight
fields green
corn grows
and the hoppers leave
for drier ground

I, too, open
as if to drink
parched from a long
spell. And today
write this poem

Angela F. Foster

CLOTHESLINE COWBOYS

On a warm windy day
I hang out the wash.
The smell of clean
mixes with sunshine.
I clothespin shirts
and jeans in a row.
Watch them dip and snap,
until they rest
in the rhythms
of a warm July breeze.

Long and lanky,
all arms and legs.
Loose limbs flutter.
Disjointed cowboys
slap each other on the back.
Yippe-ay-ky-yaying
into the wind.

Angela F. Foster

RADIO PREACHER

I'm your devil kicking, sin killing,
life bringing, Bible quoting, hell-fighting man of God

too stifling for sleep
window cracked to snag a breeze
his voice curled up the staircase
intertwined with Dad's cigarette smoke

summer humidity pulled in the signal
from Miracle Valley, headquarters for A. A. Allen
buzzing whine from kitchen Philco
louder than a thousand mosquitoes

Dad read Zane Gray, drank coffee and puffed Camels
while Reverend Allen cajoled and pleaded
renounce your sins, come to Jesus
organ music fading in and out

Don't wait, He loves you
his voice mesmerizing in the darkness
his words choking my young throat
even then I recognized
something in his voice—
familiarity with sin

Years later after Allen died during an alcoholic binge
I remembered that summer night
Even now I can almost smell my father's Camels

Candace Simar

DEVIL IN THE DETAILS

When I think of small town life I get that smothery feeling, like swallowing feathers or eating too many marshmallows at once. It's that claustrophobic closeness I experience at family reunions or when Cousin Rodney cheerfully announces he will stay an extra two weeks. I know there are those who enjoy living in small towns but I think they are the ones linked to wonderful success. Like having a brother-in-law who played in the NFL or being the daughter of the 1941 Winter Carnival Queen. Such people don't have things in their lives they'd like to forget. But it's different if you are the one remembered for failing kindergarten or throwing up during the Christmas pageant or the child of drunkards. These handicaps follow you to the grave. Like the thought of being naked in a crowd, exposed beyond comfort, no place to hide. Instinctively, I clutch my rags of individuality closer so others can't ferret out the details. Sometimes I toss out the red herring, hint that this year I'll vote Green or that I'm considering yoga classes; anything to throw them off the scent. But in a small town you can't escape. Everyone knows everything about you and your family and your kids and your great uncle and your third cousin. Nothing sacred. Nothing forgotten. It's been said the devil is in the details. The devil must feel at home in small towns. At least the ones I have known.

Candace Simar

CURTAINS

The front room curtains were crinkled plastic, bought at Ben Franklin. Country scenes of Tudor England fluttered blue and yellow in the August breeze. White linen panels in Mama's room blew straight out when the west wind howled across North Dakota, searching until it found us in Minnesota. My room faced east and the sun peeked over the lilac bushes through lavender lace, waking me each morning. I could sleep through the crowing rooster, the clatter of early breakfast before milking, the bark of Puppy herding the cows to the barn and Daddy's "Come Boss" call, but I needed the sun's touch to awaken. The gabled attic window, without any curtain at all, was my favorite spot. Wasps crawled between the panes. No matter how stifling hot or oppressive, I dared not open the storm window lest I face their stingers. I stood for hours looking beyond the barnyard, beyond Dad plowing in the farthest field, beyond the mailbox at the end of the driveway, always beyond where dreams seemed possible. I never dreamed that someday I would look back, peeking in these same windows, searching.

Candace Simar

LAST YEAR OF RURAL SCHOOL

It's a black and white day in a one-room school
chalk dust and musty books
black cats march across burlap bulletin board
hard sunlight filters through old glass
maps rolled tight like window shades
wood floors scrubbed bare by feet

Brown braids in tight tails
on either side of lips compressed to a frown
like a door closed to an October air
my expression a comment on Larry Peterson
who sits by my side for the school picture

Me, the only kid in first grade
glides down the slide on a wax paper magic carpet
swinging with Luanne, under-dog pushes from my sister
we dance the hokey-pokey on a rainy day
Mrs. Gense joins in, she smells of Paquin lotion

The Pledge of Allegiance, right hand over heart
lukewarm milk, chocolate on a lucky day
red plaid lunch box carries peanut butter on Wonder bread
after lunch we listen to Little House in the Big Woods
eyes heavy with sleep

I perch by the window on a warm radiator
trace pictures through onion paper
the drone of fifth grade Geography class behind me
never dreaming of town school
and Mrs. Paulson, who'll smack
my head with pencils
and make me
cry

Angela F. Foster

MY FATHER'S HAT

My father had a hat—brown plaid with a turned up brim. Tucked into the band, a small green feather. The last time I saw him he was wearing that hat, perched on his head at a jaunty angle.

Today in honor of my father I will wear a hat. I will perch it on my head at an angle. I will wear that hat and think of possibilities like perpetual motion. I will wonder at the power of the atom bomb. Say a curse against those damn Republicans and their farm policies. Dream of life as an ace fighter pilot during WWII. I'll walk through a farm field and admire the plantings, straight as an arrow. I will sit at the table and eat kipper snacks on crackers while reading Zane Grey. I'll tell my children stories about Indians living in the woods and the tools they made from animal bones. I will nap on the kitchen floor with my head resting against the cupboard. I will sing "Nah, Nah, Nah, Said the Little Red Fox" over and over again until my children giggle. I will tease them about a kid at school, making smoochy noises with my lips. I will give them each a fifty-cent piece and say I love them.

When the evening comes, I will throw the hat into the air and dance the one-legged jig across the lawn, remembering my father and all the good things about him. And I will wonder at the possibility of it all, if only one of his dreams had come true.

Angela F. Foster

WASHING MY FATHER'S HAIR

My father bends low over the kitchen sink
I suds small hands with lava soap
feel the grit of pumice on my fingers
stretch up on tiptoe to reach his head
water drips from elbows as I work
the lather into sweaty hair coated with grain dust
scrub curls thick as our dog Puppy's coat

Be sure to get the back of my neck, Girlie

I rub hard above his collar
glide the bar across the blackened flesh
where sweat and grease conspire
label him a dirt-farmer

Mole the size of a pencil eraser at the base of scalp
glob of shaving cream behind right ear
sunburned strip around neck and bottom
of forehead where the cap's shadow ceases

He dunks his head under the faucet and rinses soap
shakes his head like a wet dog until water splashes
the clean floor and tickles bare feet
I squeal at the unexpected coolness

he grabs a rag and towels his head, bursts
out clean and presentable for town
turns up the hems of his blue jeans and tugs laces of his good boots
shoves a check blank into his shirt pocket

I'll send you to barber college when I sell the wheat

Candace Simar

In the Middle of the Night

Hunkered at the kitchen table
plaid bathrobe and red slippers
thick glasses resting on his nose
smoke curls from dangling Camel
he sucks deep

Engrossed in turning pages
he doesn't turn his head, doesn't know I'm there
doesn't notice a mouse scurry under the refrigerator

What are you reading, Daddy?

He looks then, turns the book upside down on the table
black letters bold on the book's spine
Of Mice and Men

Candace Simar

Wonderland

The church looks smaller inside and Daddy's coffin sits off to one side like it's only there for the show and I can see his face and his hands folded across his chest, but not his feet, which are covered with a blanket like he might get cold and my aunt pulls a black comb from her purse and says how nice he looks and how he just needs to have his hair, which is usually curly, poufed up a little and he'll look like he could sit up and walk out but I know he can't, but I know he'd want to because his face is pulled into a grimace of a smile and I'm thinking he would hate to be here and I don't want to be here either and I'm thinking how flat he looks, like a balloon that has lost its air; in fact, his entire body is deflated and I wonder how he shrank or if I never noticed my whole life that he was such a small man and not really big like I thought he was or maybe there's just something wrong with me today that makes me feel like I'm Alice in Wonderland because everything looks to be the wrong size like I grew up overnight and went from a little girl to a big person and I look down at my legs and arms and wonder how they got so huge and how everything else got so terribly small.

Angela F. Foster

PLANTING TIME (A SESTINA)

Last night I dreamed my father's dream
Cultivated the soil, sowed the seed
Visualized an abundant harvest
Golden wheat shimmers in the distance
Imagined the ripeness of a south field
Before me on an August day

Last night I dreamed my father's day
Awoke to sun from a peaceful dream
Pictured the serenity of an 80-acre field
Black fertile soil ready for seed
Straight rows of wheat in the distance
The sweet hope of harvest

Last night I dreamed of harvest
Dusty wheat on an August day
Threshers working in the distance
Cool of water like a dream
Promise fulfilled of seed
Beauty of a perfect field

Last night I dreamed my father's field
Dripping heavy with harvest
Green plants stretched from seed
Ripples in the hot sun of day
Harvest before him like a dream
Heads of wheat bowing in the distance

Last night I dreamed my father in the distance
Driving his John Deere through the field
Bounty of fall a tangible dream
Sweat of his face reaps harvest
Heavy heat of an August day
Fulfillment of seed

Last night I dreamed the seed
A father's vision in the distance
Awoke to sunshine's day
Anxious for the rhythmic row of field
Dreaming of the fall harvest
As I plant his dream

Today I live his harvest, green rows in the distance
Today I sow his field, sweet promise of seed
Today I live his dream, the affirmation of a summer day

Angela F. Foster

CALLING THE NAMES

Three months before the vigil of her death, Mother sits on the single bed in her room at the Alzheimer's unit of the assisted living facility. Her short legs dangle over the edge like a child's. She pulls her winter bathrobe tight around her shrinking frame. Her short, white hair has been curled and her cheeks are a healthy pink. The room smells of urine and the Cheetos she's been snacking on.

"Do you remember Jordan?" I ask Mom, leaning forward in the recliner as I talk. Usually the mention of my youngest son's name softens her eyes and perks her up.

"No, I don't remember a Jordan," she says, shaking her head. "Do I know who that is?"

"He's my youngest boy," I say. "Don't you remember how you used to babysit for him? You were in your seventies, but you could chase after him all day."

"Yah, he's my boy," she says, but I don't see the recognition in her blue eyes.

"Jordan had school today so he couldn't come."

She nods her head like she understands but her face has the blank look I've come to recognize. "You have children, don't you?" she asks. She screws up her face as if to help her remember.

"We have four boys," I answer, knowing she has probably already forgotten the question. "Jordan is in fifth grade and James is at Bethel University. Joey and Tommy both live in Pine City. They each have a child now."

"You're married, aren't you?" Mom asks.

"Thirty years," I say. "You remember Tom, don't you?"

Mom ignores my question and opens her mouth as if she wants to ask about someone else but can't remember who. She nods her head, lost in thought. Lifts her hands and touches her index fingers together. "Linda," she says, her voice hesitating over the name of my oldest sister like she's speaking an unfamiliar language. "Claudia," she draws out the name of my second oldest sister as she taps the tip of her next finger. "Candace," she says, pushing down on her ring finger with a questioning look at me as if to make sure she has the name correct. "And then there's a boy," she adds, tapping the tip of her pinky finger. "Harold?" she shakes her head quickly. "No, that's my brother's name. It's Frank," she says, touching her finger tip again, concentrating as she repeats my brother's name. "Frankie."

"You've forgotten one really important one," I tease.

"No, I'm not done yet," she says, her voice serious as she stares down at her fingers, tapping her thumb as she searches for the name.

"Annie. That's you. My baby," she says, pointing a finger at me, a look of triumph on her face. "I've got five kids. I can't forget their names."

"It's okay, Mom. We understand if you forget. You can't help it."

"No, I have to remember." She scrunches up her face in concentration, her blue eyes intense. She touches the tips of her fingers again as she begins to repeat the process.

"Why are you so worried?" I say, reaching over to stop for a moment the movement of her hands, the calling of the names.

"I can't forget," she says, looking up from her fingers, a desperate look in her eyes. "If I forget my kids, they might forget me."

She stares back down at her hands. "Linda. Claudia." She hesitates for a moment and then continues, calling out each of her children's names as she touches her fingers. "Candace. Frank." She taps her thumb and closes her eyes for a moment in concentration. "Annie," she says looking up at me, her chin lifted, her eyes bright again for a moment. "I have five kids. I can't forget." She shakes her head. "I can't forget."

Angela F. Foster

ON OPRAH'S COUCH

"Let's write a book together," Angela said one December afternoon when we four sisters gathered for our mother's birthday party. "Can't you imagine all four of us lined up on Oprah's couch?"

We couldn't—and howled at the very idea. We were always avid readers but not one of us had attempted writing.

Angela was insistent. "Oprah gazing at us with that starry-eyed look of admiration. 'Where did you farm girls find such talent?'"

We all laughed. I must admit I didn't take Angela's idea seriously. I was busy raising teenagers and working full time. Where would I find time to write a book let alone travel to Chicago? But Angela persisted. She brought up Oprah at every holiday and in every phone conversation. "We can do it," she would say with conviction in her tone, almost making me believe.

"Linda writes the spicy parts. Claudia edits. Candy, you write the moral to the story." Angela acted like it was nothing at all. "It will be easier that way—four of us working together."

It sounded to me as if something important were missing. That we three older sisters would do all the work. "What are you going to do?"

"Oh, I'll do the rest," she said with a wave of her hand. "It can't be that hard."

Angela got me thinking. Not about Oprah, but about writing. It was something I'd always wanted to try but never had the courage. What if I failed? What if readers didn't like my work? What could I write about?

I couldn't get the idea out of my mind. I joined a local writer's group and scribbled a few short pieces for local periodicals. When my youngest daughter went off to college, I found time for a little genealogy search and discovered my great grandfather had driven the stagecoach to Fort Abercrombie shortly after the 1862 Dakota Conflict. My son challenged me to write a book about it.

I called my sisters.

"I'm starting our book," I said in an SOS broadcast. Linda had no interest writing the spicy parts. Claudia didn't offer to edit. Angela was too busy with her own kids.

And so, like the Little Red Hen, I did it on my own. Somehow I penned a first draft of *Abercrombie Trail*. It was harder than I thought. I wrote, rewrote, and signed up for more writing workshops. I couldn't find a publisher. A mentor suggested I write another book.

Pomme de Terre, my second book, became a reality. I found a publisher for my first three novels after I finished the first draft of *Birdie*. By the time *Blooming Prairie* neared completion, Claudia and Angela both helped edit. Linda, an early reader, insisted on a happy ending.

Sometimes when I'm feeling discouraged about writing, I blame my sister. After all it was Angela's fault I started all this. And yes, she's still talking about Oprah's couch. So what do you say, Oprah? Are you ready for us?

Candace Simar

FARM GIRLS KNOW

Farm girls know the alarm clock of a rooster's crow early in the morning before the sun pulls into the eastern sky, before the smell of perked coffee, before the slamming backdoor. We know cutting hay, raking hay, baling hay, stacking hay, feeding hay and the heat of the hay mow on an August day. We know all the promises: *After the chores are done. After the animals are fed. After harvest.* We know leaving family picnics before dessert and missing the county fair because of field work. We know the smell of turned soil behind the plow and the bristle of cut oats in the field. We know hay is for cattle feed, straw for bedding and if a calf comes out butt first, it's time to call Dad from the field. How a cow lowers its head to protect the new calf and the bellow of the mother after they're separated. The whoosh of the barn door as the weighted pulley yanks it shut just as our dog Puppy sidles through the narrow opening. We know a swipe of bag balm cures anything. We know how to float eggs and pull off blood suckers. The difference between a steer and a bull, a gelding and a stud, and the sound of Johnny Cash singing on the radio, the milk machines keeping rhythm. We know *don't pop the clutch* on the tractor and the tippy feel you get when driving the John Deere B. We know the grind of the stick-shift in Dad's old Dodge and the slick of gravel, just like ice, when you turn too fast. We know about forts in the lilac trees and mud pies in old tins. We know camping out like cowboys in the south pasture, our saddle a pillow for the night, horses stamping their feet behind us as we sleep. We know the cushion of oak leaves under a rope swing and the heft of our father's .22 rifle as it pings bullets into a steel target. We know the thrill of *Olly, Olly Oxen Free* and the click of fireflies in canning jars. We know *moonlight starlight, hope to see a ghost tonight.* Bare feet on dewy grass as we dart through the shadows under a butterscotch moon. We know the plume of dust that gathers to a tornado as the auctioneer's truck pulls into the farmyard. The sound of his cry as he hollers for bids. The way it feels to slide off your pony for the last time and hand over the reins. We know the din of stamping feet and drawn out *la, la, la's* as we huddle together in an empty closet, drowning out the bullet's blast as the hired man puts old Puppy down. We know the echo of the empty farmhouse's wooden floors, the hollow heels of shoes rattling our grandparents' bones in the graveyard of Tordensjold Lutheran Church. We know the way mist moves over the lake and the sound of the ducks' cry as they fly away. Farm girls know the ache of surrender as we leave the home place, the cupped-moon cradle of the farmyard's arms.

Angela F. Foster

CHILD OF ASTHMA

By the time he flips on the bedroom light,
his lips are tinted blue.
His broad shoulders bent,
in search of each raspy breath.

I toss the house, seeking the lost inhaler
under couch cushions, the pockets of empty suitcases,
the junk drawer in the hall.

My bare feet slap on the concrete drive.
Albuterol, that magic potion,
finally found beneath the car seat.
"Here it is! Here it is!" I say,
waving it above my head
like a lost teddy bear.

When he was small,
I'd stroke his soft curls.
Calm his creaky gasps, murmuring,
"Mommy's here.
   Breathe. Breathe."

And now he sucks the medicine in,
leans his head back,
eyes closed in relief.

He's almost as tall as his father.
But tonight he's my baby,
as I whisper,
   "Breathe. Breathe."

Angela F. Foster

LAST CHILD

the child
I think I am too old
to have is the one
who calls
back youth

he winds time
a backwards clock

    Tock-tick
    Tock-tick

the son who is born
as my hair turns gray
and my joints begin to ache
will watch me turn somersaults
so he can learn how

this son will coax
me to monkey play
with imaginary friends
make me giggle
hold my sides

it will be this son
who turns to me
with tear-smudged face
asks if I feel the hurt
when he skins his knee

And I will answer Yes
as I cry

It will be this son
who shares my fear
of the dark, begs to sleep
by my side
and I will let him

One night when I wake
a bad-dream scream
in my throat
just as this child screams
his dream

we will return
to slumber
snuggle
monsters not so bad
when shared

it will be this son
who causes
me to fear
passing time
the day he moves on

this son winds
time forward

    Tick-tock
    Tick-tock

as he leaves behind
a mother old

Angela F. Foster

THE FARMER'S DAUGHTERS

Sometimes I daydream about the big farmhouse of my childhood. My immigrant grandfather built it as the fulfillment of his American dream. I always loved the old place and sometimes redecorate it in my mind, hanging Grandma's antique mirror in the entryway and stripping away the carpet to reveal the hardwood floors. I replace the French doors in the dining room and restore the woodwork to its original sheen.

Every stick of wood used to build the house and barns came off the land. It's easy to imagine my grandfather cutting the timber and readying it for carpenters. Grandpa built a mansion compared to the little log cabin where they originally lived. The house built only after the barn and outbuildings were readied.

The old farm pulls at me, calls me to return to where my life began. Like a homing pigeon I dream of moving back to the place I will always call home.

While growing up, I hated outside chores. Hay bales caused an itchy rash. Oat dust made my lungs wheeze. Rats in the chicken coop sent me screaming to the house. I was afraid of the gentlest heifer. I worried about barn odors and growing too muscular. I cared more about my finger nails than picking rocks. Driving the old John Deere tractor terrified me. One wrong move and the machine might tip and roll over the hilly fields. I was not interested in stacking hay bales in neat rows or shoveling manure.

Even though I would have much rather been reading books or washing my hair, I still had to do the never ending chores. I tossed bales, scooped grain, picked rocks, washed milk machines, fed calves, cleaned calf pens, fed chickens, herded cows and did a million others tasks that needed to be done. I did them half heartedly and with great reluctance.

It always felt like spitting in the wind. In spite of my feeble efforts, I wasn't strong enough to make a difference. Dad hired a neighbor boy to help with the field work during the busy seasons. The boys never minded the barn odors or worried about the social stigma of manure on shoes. They loved to drive the tractors and machinery. It seemed easy for them.

The situation worsened with my father's first heart attack. Repeated attacks crippled him and changed him from the strong man he had been. My mother took over milking the cows morning and night. A hired man moved into our spare bedroom.

My older sisters married and left home. My younger siblings and I could not keep up with the work. The buildings slipped into disrepair. It seemed our family was treading water, waiting for the inevitable. Our roots went deep but Dad was finally forced to sell. At the time, selling was a relief. We couldn't tread water forever.

Perhaps if we four sisters had been brothers things would have turned out differently. Perhaps the home place would still be in our family, the buildings neatly tended by one of the sons who had continued our grandfather's dream.

I imagine the red-painted barn glowing in the afternoon sun and the house snug and trim. Geraniums bloom in the window boxes just like they did when Grandma was in charge. I imagine the granary filled with dusty wheat and the wooden corn crib overflowing with yellow ears. Young stock grazes in the far pasture and chickens scratch by the silo. I hear the voices of young nephews searching for kittens in the hay barn and a niece calling the cows in from the pasture. The herd plods to the barn, a long wavy line across the cow yard. Everything in place.

Just like it once was.

Candace Simar

SECRET

I love Eminem, the bad-boy rap singer. A middle-aged farm woman from small town Minnesota is not supposed to enjoy rap music. But I do. Don't get me wrong. I don't like his filthy language or the way he talks about minorities. I like the beat of the music and the words that keep coming in sharp staccato fashion. I try to be strong and listen to oldies or country western, but then the Eminem urge strikes me. The rhythms, the words, they just get to me. I daydream about Eminem. I'd like to invite him over for Sunday dinner. I'll use the good dishes and make a pot roast with gravy. I bet he hasn't had real mashed potatoes with butter in years. I'll make a green jell-o salad with tiny marshmallows and my special bundt cake for dessert. After dinner, I'll play the piano and we can make some nice words for his rap songs. I'll talk to him about his language. I'm sure he's a good boy at heart.

Angela F. Foster

PRAIRIE

Dream with me
I dreamed the purple evening sky
dream with me
I dreamed the paths where geese would fly
I dreamed a dream for you

Rise with me
stretch wingtips to the skies
angels hide in prairie winds
lifting you still higher
these servants flames of fire
come dream with me

Soar with me
glide over open plains
release your spirit, dare to dream
I dreamed this moment that I bring to you
I dreamed this moment that I sing to you
come dream with me

Candace Simar

Lilacs

LILAC TIME

Lavender cone heads
fragrantly slurping
from old pickle jars
on every
kitchen table
in town.

Candace Simar

LETTING GO

After your funeral
we gather on the steps
of the Lutheran church, blue
and white balloons clutched
in our shaking hands

one by one we release
them to the sky
the ribboned strings
sliding from our
reluctant fingers

We crane our necks
to watch the last
speck disappear
in the winter sky
wondering

what's to come
of those you left
behind
our breath brief
in the cold, cold air

Angela F. Foster

YOU NEVER KNOW

My older sister Linda
who speaks with me
on the phone at least
twice a week

and visits so often she feels
comfortable enough to rummage
through my fridge and complain
about the lack of cream for her coffee

phoned this morning to say
she was just thinking about me
and decided she should call
to tell me she loves me

because
you know
you never know

and when I told her
I loved her too
she cried

Angela F. Foster

RECIPE FOR SOUP

If the weather is nice
enough to hang out
your laundry
don't make soup

Save it for days
with a nip in the air
or at least a sky
that's overcast

Start the soup
as soon as you wake
have plenty of carrots
celery and onions

Never hurry. Pause often
to read a good book
sing as you chop onions
call your sister
while mixing dumplings

You'll know the ingredients are right
if you step outside. If it doesn't smell
good when you walk back in,
it won't taste good either

You'll always
need to add
something more
probably carrots

The real secret to soup
is something in the oven
bread is best
cake or homemade pie will do

Expect everyone who walks
in your door to head straight
for the stove. They'll give
the soup a stir and ask for a taste

Be generous. Share
with everyone you know
pour the soup
into glass jars

Hold your soup to the light
admire the dumplings
the small bits of carrots
those green peas floating in broth

Angela F. Foster

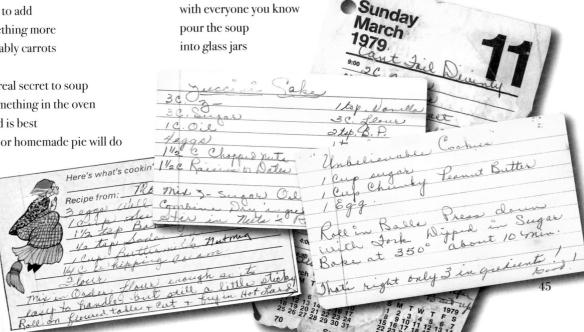

45

MOTHER WITH ALZHEIMER'S

a boat

   she is
tethered in choppy waters

when the wind
       picks up

I'll rest
  my tired arms

drop
  my useless lines

watch
      her drift
          alone
out to
sea

Angela F. Foster

MOTHER'S DAY 2011

The grandfather clock
chimes twelve times in the hallway
the oak dresser fills the empty
wall, its mirror reflects the wedding portrait
hanging by the door

The crystal pitcher
gleams on the hand-crocheted table cloth
draping the antique, claw-foot table
Depression Glass cradles her recipes

Her things mingle
easily with ours
On this first Mother's Day without her
I reach for the gravy boat
curl my fingers around its handle

Candace Simar

WE WAITED TOO LONG

Towards the end
old folks live
in sputters and spurts
a good day, a couple bad ones

Fretting over lost keys
and the cost of butter
worn bony with effort
to keep up appearances

When their time comes
they leave without complaint
weary enough to sink into the first
good sleep they've had in years

They leave to us our inheritance
small slips of paper, notes we can't decipher
black and white photos of forgotten faces
recipes we'll never make

The ones left behind talk about
things they should have asked
say at the funeral
we waited too long

Angela F. Foster

STILL IN THE GAME

You should have seen her at forty—
skating backwards
graceful as the letter S.

At fifty, she bought
a mini-bike and a snowmobile.
Living life like a dare.

At sixty she slid down the giant
slide at the State Fair—whooping
and hollering all the way down.

We almost lost
her at sixty-eight—
heart attack, quintuple by-pass.

But today
she plays HORSE
with her youngest grandson.

White head bobbing
as she chases the ball. Arms
outstretched like she can stop time.

He sinks it and she throws short,
H! he call outs. Dribbles. Giggles. *O*!
as he lands another and she misses. *R, S*!

He bends in glee. Anticipates
an easy win. Points to the spot.
You have to make it from here or you lose.

She stoops over
the ball. Dribbles
with concentration.

Shoots with arms
frail as dandelion froth.
Sinks it. Claps her hands.

Hoots with joy.
Grandma at eighty
Still in the game.

Angela F. Foster

LIVING BREATH, DYING BREATH

"All poems are done with the dying breath. Language on the inhaled
breath is rare.... it is the language of grandmothers." Li-Young Lee

My grandmother knew this language
the language of the inward breath. As all Norwegians
she sucked in her breath with ya on her lips

It was the word to fill a pause, the vocabulary
of acceptance, of knowing there was nothing
to do but make coffee and get busy
doing something else. It was the ya

spoken when Grandpa spent grocery money at the tavern
when sons left for war, when children died
when my sister had a baby
before the wedding

The universal grandmother language
acknowledges life goes on
even when things go wrong. Ya
on the exhaled breath gives an answer. Ya

on the inward breath
tells nothing
gives nothing
offers nothing

Though a poem may ride
the dying breath, one also clings
to that haunting
inward gasp
      Ya

Candace Simar

Farm Girls **49**

Barn Coats

Her skin hangs like an old barn coat, draped and bunched in all the wrong places. Worn out, reduced only to needs, Mom poses with jutted hip for balance, tilting her head like I remember Grandpa doing. Her stance reminds me of gummed black-and-white pictures in ancient photograph albums. I never noticed their resemblance until these last years as her flesh has fallen away and her blue eyes float like circles of sky behind thick glasses. I never thought to compare them, he with his beer-tainted breath and pockets of Sen-Sen, she with her wild ways and betrayal of Dad. In a rush of middle-aged wisdom, I see how much alike they are. My father's barn coat hung in the mud room of our farmhouse, worn only to the milking parlor or calf pens, until his heart finally burst under the strain. Buried young in his Sunday best.

Candace Simar

KINGDOM

I dream of dirt—black, rich and fertile. The dirt my father spent a lifetime working. Every spring my father spent long hours in the field, cultivating and planting. Evenings, he would come in for supper, his shoulders slumped with fatigue and his eyes rimmed black with dirt. He would scrub his hands and face at the kitchen sink with a stiff bristle brush, lathering Lava soap up his arms and along the collar of his shirt.

Every morning he would be back on the tractor as soon as the milking was finished. At noon, I would run through the field, my pigtails flying, with a Mason jar of coffee, sandwiches wrapped in wax paper and Mom's homemade doughnuts still warm from the fryer. Dad would see me coming and stop the John Deere. We would lean against the big tire as he ate, his fingers smearing black dirt across the white bread. He would drink the lukewarm coffee straight from the jar and loop the doughnut over his index finger as he pulled himself onto the tractor seat.

"Bring more doughnuts and some coffee in a few hours, will you?" Dad would say before throwing the still-humming tractor into gear as he motioned for me to move back so he could begin another tedious round on the field.

By summer's end, Dad's face and neck were a dark-red color from hours in the sun, his seed cap creating a white tan line across his forehead. When he fired up the tractor or sat on the swather to cut hay, he was king of the world. A handful of dirt run through his fingers and a glance into the sky would tell him when the fields were ready for seed. He knew when the grain was ripe for harvest and the hay dry enough to bale. He wasn't afraid of the bull, the cow that had just given birth, or the lightning that flashed across the sky during a rainstorm.

Summer months, when the dairy cattle pastured on the north end of the farm almost a mile from home, Dad would stand in the doorway of the barn, his hands cupped around his mouth and yell, "Come boss! Come boss!" His voice was magic. Soon those brown Jersey cows would walk single-file down the narrow dirt trail, their full bags swinging as they wound their way through the green pasture, the same trail used by generations of cattle before them. They traveled neatly, never deviating from that long snake-like dirt trail that wound its way around boulders and trees, puddles and ravines. The cows were one organized line all the way back to the farm and the sound of my father's voice.

Dad was proud of a well-planted field. Saturday morning trips to town Dad would drive slowly, rubbernecking the neighbor's crops. He would shake his head in disgust at the farmer who still had not planted his corn well into the month of June or the man who sowed his wheat in wobbly, uneven lines. He saved his praise for the farmer who took pride in even, perfect rows. "Just look at those crops," my father would say. "Straight as an arrow."

Dad was still in his 40s when his heart weakened from hard work. When I was twelve years old, Dad signed the papers to sell the farm to a new family. The attic was cleared of the trunks my grandparents had saved, full of old papers and clothing. Mom swept the scratched oak floors of the house and scrubbed the old porcelain kitchen sink for the last time. Our crippled dog Puppy was put down and the chickens we couldn't catch, abandoned. Almost everything we owned was listed on an auction bill, and on a Wednesday in June 1970, our equipment, livestock, and most of our furniture was sold in bits and pieces to the highest bidder.

The biggest loss was the dirt itself, the land my grandparents had farmed. The land my father had lived on since birth. The land my generation wasn't able to keep.

I wish I could go back to the home place and walk those fields again. See my father stand in the barn door. Hear his voice loud and low calling, "Come boss! Come boss!" If I could stand there for a moment, I would pretend the Jersey cows were coming down the path, ready for the evening milking. I would get my fingernails black and my shoes full of dirt picking rocks. I would hoist a bale of green alfalfa just to remind myself of how scratchy and heavy the squares are. I would check the sky for any sign of rain and run a handful of that black dirt through my fingers. I would look out over the freshly plowed fields like I was king of the world—take a deep breath of it, and dream for a moment it was all still mine.

Angela F. Foster

Acknowledgements

Our sincere appreciation to the editors of the following publications in which some of these poems were first published:

The Moccasin, Talking Stick, Dust and Fire, Lake Country Journal, Poetry Midwest, County Lines, Talking Seventh Street Blues, Ottertail Review, and *Encore.*

A special thank you to Penny Swanum for her helpful critique.

Candace is a grateful recipient of Five Wings Arts Council grants with funds from the McKnight Foundation. Angela acknowledges a grant from East Central Arts Council, funded in part by the McKnight Foundation.

Living Breath, Dying Breath epigraph was quoted from a 2004 lecture given by Li-Young Lee at Calvin College in Grand Rapids, Michigan.

Authors

Angela F. Foster and Candace Simar are sisters. Raised on a second generation farmstead, they will always think of their childhood farm in Ottertail County, Minnesota, as home.

Angela, a poet and memoirist, teaches creative writing at the Loft Literary Center in Minneapolis and lives on a farm in rural Pine City, Minnesota. Angela claims bragging rights as the Pie Poet Laureate of Braham Pie Days and has the apron to prove it.

Candace, a writer and poet from Pequot Lakes, Minnesota, carries a passion for Minnesota history and her Scandinavian heritage. She is the author of *The Abercrombie Trail Series: Abercrombie Trail* 2009; *Pomme de Terre* 2010; Spur-Award winning *Birdie* 2011; and *Blooming Prairie* 2012. Candace's claim to fame is receiving first, second and third place in the Hackensack Art's Fair poetry contest, the year she had the only submission.

www.AngelaFFoster.com/
www.CandaceSimar.com/